On Trust: A Book

Also by James Womack from Carcanet

Misprint
'Vladimir Mayakovsky' And Other Poems (translations)

JAMES WOMACK

ON TRUST
A Book of Lies

'True?' said the Colonel. *'Of course my stories are true.
They may not have happened in quite this way, or at quite
this time, or even to quite these people. But they're all true.'*

Cupid implies; Venus infers.

CARCANET

Some of these poems have appeared in *PN Review*, *Salon of the Refused*, *Under the Radar*, *In my Basket I Dream: The University of Reading Creative Arts Anthology 2016* and *New Poetries V*. Six of these poems were published in the limited edition Desperate Literature pamphlet *Richard Scott / James Womack* (Madrid, 2017). Spanish versions of six poems have been published in *Quimera*. The translation of 'error' by Marianna Geide is included by kind permission of the author. The translation of 'Europa' by Marie Luise Kaschnitz is included by kind permission of Graf & Graf.

First published in Great Britain in 2017 by
Carcanet Press Limited
Alliance House, 30 Cross Street,
Manchester, M2 7AQ

www.carcanet.co.uk

A CIP catalogue record for this book is
available from the British Library,
ISBN 978 1 784104 16 0

Typeset in Great Britain by XL Publishing, Exmouth, Devon
Printed in Great Britain by SRP Ltd., Exeter, Devon

The publisher acknowledges financial
assistance from Arts Council England.

Contents

AUTHOR BIOGRAPHY

Oh none of this ever happened, but one feels so grown-up composing a self out of details not entirely meritworthy.

'FLEW IN ON NEW YEAR'S DAY THE FIREWORKS'

flew in on New Year's Day the fireworks
beneath my plane like sudden lichen

my wife uses a caviar jar for an ashtray
wants her tombstone to read FINALLY JUSTICE

one neighbour is losing her mind the doorbell
often rings as she goes to look for herself

taking my arm in her hand and angry
asking again and again why do you live here

TARGET

I'd like to be a queen of people's hearts...

Bored at ourselves, we filled bottles both glass and plastic with the
undrinkable tap water.
We opened the large window and took a five paces run-up.
The bottles all burst. Some burst subtly, a disappointing collapse
and split.
Others burst beautifully in a corona of shrapnel round a
surprisingly dry centre.
This was the fourteenth floor, the fag-end of August, years and years
ago.
The supervisor was alerted by the crashing the cheers the who-
knows-what.
He came to our door smoking a cigarette.
*Listen, you little cunts, if you throw more shit out of the window you're
for it.*
What, us? We haven't been doing anything. Look, the window is closed.
Hmph. So you didn't throw anything? No. We did not think he was
convinced.
I will take photos and prove the truth one way or another.
A day or so of tension, him refusing to speak to us or to unlock the
washing machine.
But then on the last day of the month he was grumpy but somehow
tender.
I am sorry about your princess. But she was a liar as well.

THAT KISS

Nobody noticed, except the two who were meant to notice,
as the rapid ritual greeting, left cheek, right cheek,
was prolonged ever-so ever-so slightly
and one breathed in close on the curve of the other's jaw.

CO-RESPONDENT

That morning, N and the baby being asleep,
I sat down to write a rebuttal to one of your love-letters.
But you know how it is:
you set out to perform some ordinary task,
to buy the bread, maybe, or else *I won't be long,*
just taking the videos back to the shop,
and then round a corner
the full majesty of the goddess Freya
strikes you in the face and blinds you.
Which was how it was. I cannot live in this world,
the goddess of beauty and death lounging
at street corners. Was this what I meant to write?
Anyway, I never took the videos back.
One of them was 'our film', if you remember,
or don't think it odd that shared possessions
are alleged to define or fix relationship.
'Our song', of course, is *Yakety Sax*,
but the film behind my eyes admits of any soundtrack—
your hair wet from the pool, a night that smelt of ozone.
And although my dream of you
is not the same as you,
it is in fact love, it is love.
Write that often and it will be enough.

SUCH AFFAIRS

About such affairs it is easier to be ironic than just
but one senses a grand disjuncture
between our nights in the tearful hotels
and their never-so-resonant souvenirs:
soap, bath foam, coat hangers, a sewing kit.

SEAWIFE

That summer of flesh-coloured jelly shoes
I lost my wedding ring,
a ring with a line on it like a line of surf,
and I lost it in the sea.

A hopeless day later I went to the shore
and found, half-buried at the tideline
with the sun growing on it,
another ring, not mine.
A battered silver ring
where I could not see my face.
Against the advice of every fairy-tale
I put it on, and now am lost.

Day and night I hear her voice:
in the storms when she comes
to command vainly against the rocks,
or more insidious, in the kiss
of foam on sand, bare now, not boastful.
She calls me and I go:
in two minutes I can be inside her.

And what about my fleshwife?
It carries on as normal, tidal,
but I think of the sea as I fuck her,
kiss the tears from her face, for the salt.
Each morning I leave bed early
and walk the shoreline
waiting for messages: marks in the sand,
the seabirds' clumsy cuneiform.

I.

I travel with people I love
to visit people I tolerate
and think about people I love:
it's almost a riddle.
As the Sphinx asked,
what animal grows a third leg
simply by thinking about you?

II.

The old chivalric rules.
The lovers show their purity:
they are to share a single bed, naked,
and never touch.
I must be the purest lover left alive.

III.

Writing academic papers
on *The Significance of the Orgasm*;
all the time thinking
if you've gotta ask, you'll never know.

NOTE TO SELF (I)

It's simple, I'm sorry.
It's not you, it's me.

TO * * * *

Pour me a beer, and I'll remember my geography.
No, I know this city: the darks and the lights of it,
the Space Tower consulates, the summer-rancid metro,
the woman by the emergency ward at midnight—
her phone held so it looks as though her heart were glowing—
or the midnight buses like ultraviolet aquariums.
Pour me a beer... I know this city, these lives
that jog past in the park, unobtainable as storefront cherries.
And I could sit here a long time, long as the journey
from the affluent north down to the mirror-sweating avenues.
I know this city like your hand on my back.
Pour me a beer, I could sit here forever.
An owl flies past, hooting *oy vey, oy vey.*

AISLING

I.

Without the use of magic urine, sacred fungus,
strange distilled rainbows,
she came to me, not as I had dreamt,
but as I lay dreaming.

She came silently as a nightmare woman,
across the apocalyptic plains of Las Suertes,
through Pirámides, Mira el Sol,
her feet never touching the ground.

Up the eighty-six stairs
to the flat in Faith Street
to lodge finally in my hot bed
in my tousled amygdala.

She was tiny, and vast as a country,
a ragged comb stuck in her loose hair
her legs dusty to the calves
her dress, impeccable.

II.

And it was like eavesdropping against loud music,
twenty crossing voices in a bar
all from the same mouth, imploring—
too much of this would madden anyone—

she saw my distress and smiled,
spoke clear above the hubbub,

her voice affectionate,
cool on my brain.

And my mouth closed up
my lips were sewn with strange threads.
She took both halves of our discussion
adding me to the babble she already ruled.

My tongue caught against the cunning sutures.
Her skin was transparent now in her brown arms
and against the warm dome of her skull.
I could see her teeth through her lips.

III.

For a moment she was old,
old as a burnt forest,
old as a stone.
And she spoke on, spoke all night until

my lips untied and her brown eyes closed on my brain,
and the certain smile
was the last thing I saw before waking
bare and ready for creation.

I.

A.   We met at the inadequate garden I remember
the benches rotten, sodden, sprouting in parts
with a young shoot pushed up through a knothole.
Our feet soaked from the grass—we almost waded.

B.   But you had plucked a sprig of honesty and braided
a necklace a crown a loop, I don't remember,
and looked at me through the new-made hole
with a smile—one hand to stop it flying apart.

C.   Lie with me. Your eyes smiling—my heart
audible almost above everything I said.
My hand on your arm, your breath steady and slow.
All these details...you remember?

D.   You said *Yes I remember it well. But these parts
are more than their whole and the honesty has faded.*

II.

A.   We met in the staid café—leaf tea and cucumber
sandwiches. You were before me, your notes
spread out in a Maginot Line on the table.
You kept me quiet and waiting till you ordered.

B.   Did you lie to me? The memory has faded,
hardened over, like resin hardens to amber.
And I do not care if you were playing a role,
that all you said wasn't from the heart.

C.   The summer makes old wounds smart—
no past is ever gone, it only plays dead
then gets up behind you from a bolt-hole
with its reminder: *For you, Tommy, ze affair is over.*

D.   Ah well, an affair to remember...No need to be hurt,
you're not *ill*. Thank you madam, the agony is abated.

III.

A.   This was your bedroom, and outside, September.
     The planet cooling and the radiator hot.
     We undressed as fast as we were able,
     fingers misbehaving on every button they undid.

B.   But all the time that lay before us splendid
     with hope and delay and tender castles in the air...
     Who cares if they are crumbled down to rubble?
     They had their delicate spires and oubliettes.

C.   We did not move until there was no more light
     and we had to move, went out amid
     the shopfronts and the taxis and the people
     holding hands, the evening without number.

D.   There was fire, and now, embers. We part
     and the pale moon blushes to be so outdated.

IV.

A.   The trees were empty and there was snow here.
Our hands were red and sore with the regret
that to be alone together was more desirable
than to be warm or otherwise comforted.

B.   And your eyes were close and guarded...
But thoughts of that time outnumber
and overwhelm me, with the whole
crop of fruitlessness itemised and set out.

C.   An afternoon whose details lie unannounced
in me, which returns to me unexpected
and causes my heart to turn and close
if sad stray thought makes me remember.

D.   We pass and clamber through all impediments.
All shall be well when the pain has faded.

Last week, as he hovered against the border of an unmentionable bourgeois transgression (I would have written *transaction*, I did, I did write *transaction*, it seemed to fit in well, but no, *transgression*, *transgression*; and *bourgeois*, certainly, just to be sure, we are not talking about the kind of sin that we do, no doubt erroneously, keep in our minds as a moral marker—no one has ever excused or exculpated this, ejaculating into the anus of a six-year-old- girl, for example—but another kind of sin, one that hurts, but obliquely: that might damage your social status, prevent your child from getting into his first-choice school, depress house prices in your suburb, a minor sin perhaps, but in time forgettable, and *unmentionable* is naturally a lie, what are we doing now if not talking about it, *unmentionable* is a hangover; so that's that all cleared up, onwards), sleeping with one of his students (so how close was he to this border, this so-called *unmentionable* border; he assumed, rightly as future events would show, that she would reciprocate the vague lust he felt when he talked to her casually after classes, and that the signs she gave him, maintaining her gaze and licking her lips more often than was warranted by the weather or the air-conditioning, laughing slightly loud and feeling the labia minora swell and redden, were indeed signs rather than misread coincidences), he stood in his office watching the clouds tear and knit.

Enough. Heading home one last time,
he saw a leaf fall dark against the dark sky
and the black branches, and then decide
it was a bird, and perch above his head.

The arguments he used to justify toying with the idea in the first place, the idea of the absolute limit, that events do not exist until they actually happen, now came back to bump against *if thine eye offend thee* (better advice) in his dulled and satisfied and unhappy and aroused mind, now that *why not cross this boundary* had become less a skirt to push against and finally tear and more of a reproach which developed its different and seemingly final emphasis the more he thought about it, at the same time as less relevant (I would have written *reverent*, I could have) ideas swam into shape, how to tell her for instance, what form to give the truth, his first thought was *I have something to expiate: hepatitis*, a terrible pun of the kind they had laughed at but he realised, or had known for some time, that his life was made of lines drawn in the sand by some finger or other and that jokes and puzzles and tendernesses were no longer available, or were boxed away for the indefinite attic future of hotels and bathrooms; for it is the architecture that alters when we provoke change, and for some time we look into rooms that are no longer there, share space with people who live in it at different times at different rates, miss the past and call for him *who calleth those things which be not as though they were*, a marriage a marriage, a marriage. He was stone quiet until he broke and sobbed. *'My house has no walls.' 'Really? How does it smell?'*

DICK JOKES

everything I write is an approximation to that face...

So here we are, cakewalking on the edge of the abyss,
for no reason other than that an email must have been lost.
I'm writing this replacement
in a poker-players' convent,
though it makes no difference. You do not now exist.

I tried to describe you to friends. The closest I got
was *it's a kind of a parlour trick face; curling eyebrows,*
either an old lady
or a rabbit... Not doing very well, am I?
I nicknamed you Gift Horse, because you let me come in your mouth.

But then again, I called my penis Metonymy, a part for the whole,
so it's not like I can be trusted. Parts of me can't be trusted.
You made a mistake in the first place;
you backed your own terrible horse.
Who hasn't dreamt of unearned winnings? These fingers are rusty.

And now I try by thought alone to carry myself where you are.
But I don't even know the options, and what if I get it wrong?
Saddle up, ride through the curving night,
you still won't overtake an email in its flight.
In your park, the wind pushes at an empty swing.

As always, and just like that, the smell of sandalwood still
stops me still. And the only way to dull the noise of the dead
is to put your head underwater
and hold it there. *One. Two. Three. Four.*
How close am I? This close: an invisible man sleeping in your bed.

Who you gonna call? But again: *seen one phoenix, seen 'em all.*
And you are gone away: frozen Netflix can't cover that up.
We both write our own manifestoes:
you only exist if I interact with you.
But the cost! Such expense would make divorce look cheap.

Armies have marched through these testicles, a grunting invasion.
Metonymy is the thing that never knows its place.
I have sent this email to myself it
is true. And: I used my penis as a selfie
stick—*so that's what the earth looks like from space!*

(This is, like, *so* untrue.) You rang my mobile, asked *what are we?*
All your memes are judging you; you know that in your bones.
But we have to live here,
at the permanent edge of thunder:
the conscious and the unconscious; the river on its bed of stones.

LISTEN, FRIDAY WAS CRAZY

Whoever looked into the mirror drunk
had for a moment to see that flicker—
the hovering ghost of truth
silent between himself and the reflection—
that even the exact copy is untrustworthy;
someone else's eyes, you're imitating yourself.
But what do I know? Look, Friday was crazy...
Now: the clouds like dumplings in a soup-blue sky.

Then, the black skirts of my umbrella;
that grey-white frou-frou, rain over the mountain.
A great sign that your heart is burning
when one will not do so much as look at another.
So how could we not then talk about the weather?
and gradually hide ourselves in the thicker trees
as the rain rolled up with its meaningless fairground patter.
But, we do not admire the rain for its eloquence.

'DO YOU REMEMBER A COUPLE OF POEMS BACK'

Do you remember a couple of poems back
when I was talking about dreams?
Last night I didn't sleep at all—
too much iced tea and loneliness.
Instead in a sort of daze I thought of the dark
of the green light from the radio display
and remembered that woman—
dancing with her and the tequila sharp in me.
Or did I read this somewhere? Will the morning come?

I said that it had been destroyed—
I swore to her by Marie Lloyd—
and yes, she's bound to be annoyed,
    mad as a spider,
but I kept the porno Polaroid
    of me inside her.

Set out to find traces of him from the last known point heading in
the four cardinal directions to try to find

we are lucky, go north, meet first people who took his gold, then
clothes and gun, finally come across him himself

lying dead with only his good works in his fingers

the loss of objects follows clear patterns like the stages of any relation
have I ever moved state sober climbed from one energy band to the
next

said fuck it in the middle of a boring evening's entertainment and
ducked out moved giggling behind the blackout curtains her hand
in my hand

swipe to dismiss

the white body, the white snowdrifts

How did they meet? By chance, like everyone.
What were they called? Why should you care?
But one morning, round about midnight,
she nudged him awake and said, 'Are you asleep?
Come upstairs, the sea's like a mirror.'
He grumbled a little, but got dressed and followed.

Back then the whole world was mildly erotic
when he looked at it; he needed to see it through her.
From upstairs, indeed, the sea was like a mirror,
though he didn't really want to look at the sea.
Where were they coming from? Somewhere close.
Where were they going? Who ever knows that?

More scenes from recumbent life: he sits in bed
with his figleaf notebook; she wanders round the room,
naked, deadheading potplants. 'What are you doing?'
she asks. 'Trying to sketch you,' he replies.
She comes over, interested, and peers at the page,
and then, with a shrug: 'But these are just words!'

The coin falls on its edge, if it falls at all.
Long afterwards, they woke him again
and said, 'Hey, come out onto the roof,
the sea's amazing!' He followed before he remembered,
and the sea was indeed like a mirror.
He looked into it, and saw nothing look back.

NOTE TO SELF (II)

The calls are coming from inside the house...

As heart turns the blood in its inconclusive circle.

That one evening I too could sit on the porch, the cat burring against my thumb like a burnt man breathing through gauze. Inside the house they are picking through Debussy, a composer new to the prairie in 1920.

That an uninterrupted walk is one act with respect to its moral genus, but it can happen that it is many moral acts, if the will of the walker alters, will being the principle of moral acts.

That memories are made of milk.

That adultery does not exist; the phrase you misheard was, every woman *has* a love triangle.

That Arial is a fairy who is help to Prospero, her features "purity, innocence" are the opposite to Carnival, who is very unpleasant.

That thers no doubt. but mercy may be found yf yo^u so seek [yt].

That the men of the past were dragons and phoenixes, and you are nothing but crickets and butterflies, the ghosts of crickets and butterflies!

That here the green and yellow sadlands are occasionally broken by vast machines that grade the sand. Hour-glass, beach, boxing-ring.

That she's dancing, but even when she dies she's dancing.

That any writing about the city has no single author; I repeat, any writing has no single author.

That if a figure is repeated it may be more beautiful than when it is only seen once. But here I am, talking about jewellery...

LETHE

a colourless river
who drains the savour
from the herbs that edge her

black poppies
black rosemary
black forget-mes

The naked Fates occupy a lending-library in Madrid—
no one uses it, no requests are sent.
They sit naked in the bookish gloom, in the three darkest
corners, knitting between them some vast shawl.
    One to measure, one to mark and one to cut.
For the traditional fee in this vaulted hall you may examine
the images they cast into the growing tissue.
    One to measure, one to mark and one to cut,
and from whom no secrets are hid...
The fabric spreads like a carnivorous plant.
    One to measure, one to mark and one to cut.
If you speak to them they will ask you what it was you said
to be sure they understand what you meant
but then they will show you i.e. these figures from your past

you needed to see—how they live, are they living still,
where they found happiness, what shores they haunt...
They exchange secrets for secrets, so get it all off your chest—
tell them why you came, tell them what you have lost, tell it all.
    One to measure, one to mark and one to cut.
They can give you the contact details of the dead,
and point out the loose ends you will want to pull
    (*One to measure, one to mark and one to cut*)
as if that would help, to unravel things. I have heard
of people in the same position as I am, intent
on discovering their past discretions, ones they lost,
who have sought them through the labyrinth of chat-room threads,
managed to touch them with a virtual hand.
                          what do you want?
to sleep with you again
           to be honest

UNTITLED

The Marquis de Sade's receptions are noted in society
for their host's exquisite taste that captivates his guests.
'Why, Marquis, with this large unlubricated butt plug
you are really spoiling me.'

to me it will not be granted to take shelter within your two doors that open like wings, in this haughty building with no awnings and no annexes; I key in the code which used to be my name, and it replies: *error*, and I say yes, I got it wrong, I got it wrong, but it repeats: *error*, and I say yes, I made a mistake, I made a mistake, and the only door that I could knock at was your door, but it says: *error*, and as for me, what is left to me now, to wait, to stick like a shadow to some approaching homeowner or guest, and hope that he does not ask: where are you going? who are you going to see? what, really, is it that you need? and I cannot lie and say that I live here, because by my greasy clothes, by my broken nails, by my puffy face—a drunken face down to the very skull—by all these it is clear to anyone that I do not live anywhere: not here, not anywhere else.

within your two doors like wings folded after flight. under your two hundred eyes, which burn for several hours and then die out as the night goes on. this building where I once could stay. the building where there were more doors than doorways, because each doorway held two or three doors: the iron door, the wooden door, the glass door, the tin door, the imagined door, the invisible door... and some of them had an eye that looked outwards, and some of them had an eye that looked inwards, and some were locked from the outside, and some of them were not locked at all, and for others it was as though their keys had been lost, and some had never had keys, because they recognised people by their face or by their fingerprints, and all the same I never managed to penetrate far enough, and I raged and I laughed and I hurt, but I could never believe that I would stand so completely outside, right in the street, with greasy clothes, with broken nails, with a head dull and light as a baseball bat, because there is nothing for it now than to beat, beat, beat against this door which is as closed as the eye of a man asleep, closed as the grave, closed as a pair of wings, as the cataclysm, as the gates of kings, as the credit card I used to take out and misspend all my money, closed as the first syllable of the word *error* and closed as the last syllable of the word *error*.

after the Russian of Marianna Geide

And then you ask,
how can this page you translate be about you?
Aren't another's words truly prophylactic,
even when lifted into your own words?
But—inference objection—your own words,
are they always yours, or always you?
When I see the eyes I've tattooed on my own eyes...
(Though someone else had to say even that first.)

NOTE TO SELF (III)

You thought that you knew me
but this is the new me:
I'm not what you wanted?
Go ahead, sue me...

In the undesired side of the park where no one goes
but the joggers, I found myself one green morning.
The shade spread over me as I walked under the arching trees,
and I tried to take a photograph, photographs,
of the chiaroscuro in the sprinkler
as it threw water in and out of patches of sunlight.
All I succeeded in noting was an anamorphic stain,
a brushstroke that squint as I might I could not
resolve into anything coherent, a skull.
Then a group of joggers ran through me, heads down,
refusing to swerve, bustling me out of the way.
Oi, you fuckers! I'm in the arcades too! I yelled after them,
then, *Go on, you run, as much as you like, you'll never get far enough.*

'I KISS YOU ONCE AND SAY *I LOVE YOU* TWICE'

I kiss you once and say *I love you* twice,
once in the large room and once by the door
that sticks and needs to be argued open and shut;
now I've bullied it open, and I pause at the threshold,
pushing back the cats with my boots and my bag,
and *I love you* I call down the hall to the large room
and although you don't call back *I love you*, you do say *'bye*,
casually, just as you'd offered your cheek to be kissed
and I look down the corridor and though I can't see you
I know you are there and I think *That's enough*
and I'm in the world and you are there in the warm
and there's much more between us than this reluctant door.

The young are not fully awake for the first year,
and so glass puzzles them and makes them curious.
They enjoy the reflection, doubled reflection
in train windows, peer out through the two reflections,
staring down the fog, and faded sodden landscape,
and a few shy trees... Eager breath on the glass.
Other signs of excitement: smiles as the light breaks
in a glass of water, reaching out to mirrors.
They live on other boundaries as well—sometimes
I have seen an unclear mischievous spirit poised
in the doorway. That must be his little white ghost,
silent as a white weasel, who leaves the sleeping
body and explores the house. Once I caught its eye:
it held my locked gaze fearlessly for a second,
then sprang to the crib. He pulled himself from sleep,
then stretched out one arm, like an amateur Macbeth
looking for his dagger. The next day in the shower
he laughed to lift his hand under the showerhead,
wanting to catch and hold the warm transparent lines.

FORESHADOWING

All his life, my son has slept in our bed, for immediate, at times it seems exclusive, access to my wife. Recently, he has started to kick out at me, pushing me to the edge of the mattress. Most nights I have to lie straight as a poker. To prevent my arms dangling over the edge of the bed, I cross them, lay them out over my belly. When I can't sleep, I think of the future.

From here, the sun is broad as a human foot.
Red wine in your fridge, and you're blushing at your life,
your entire life, an embarrassing, constantly-threatened secret
(think e.g. the man who was fucking his sister
when he heard that Kennedy had been shot).
A provincial anecdote: you say to yourself
that normal people need draft after draft
to get their stories straight.
You say this to yourself, you say this surprisingly often.
Summer of St Michael, quince summer, archangel summer.
The last Sunday in October.
Beep beep beep, this year is reversing.
Fire on its approach will judge and condemn us all.

NOTE TO SELF (IV)

your life
is a leaf:
every autumn
it burns...

You in Switzerland, walking away from a divorce,
but you lent me your flat for a night—*or as long as
it takes, James*—and I am here like the ghost,
putting what I remember of you two together.
Dust in the city kills everything. I strike
an accidental chord from your decorative piano,
and think I have woken the rats—
at least, something scuttles in the cabinets.
In the fridge, an orange on the glass shelf
rhymes imperfectly with its own reflection.
I too do not like to spend much time with myself:
before I go to sleep I stand at your windows
and look across to the student dorms—
see what happens where the lights for now
imagine the neutral territory, the unlit rooms.

In love, for anger is a kind of love,
I took the metro to the northern suburbs
and escaped to dust, to buildings in collapse,
blocks upon blocks of them dominoing down.
I thought it was my fault; the rage compacted
at the speartip of the train as it pushed into the station.
But who is that important, or that cross?
Then I saw the sign hung across the road,
the smirking mayor with his thumbs up and the slogan
Así arranca una nueva época.

This is how each new epoch begins,
with steel and concrete cast down into rubble
and a man with his thumbs up telling us to rejoice.
A new start every few years, because the others got it wrong.
If you loved me we would have apples
you'd said at our argument's absurd climax
and I half-slammed the door as I left
and then rode as far as I could but no further.
A new-build wasteland where anything could happen:
I felt foolish and suddenly small and erratic.

We have all too often been woken from pleasant dreams.
I found a Chinese grocery for the apples:
your favourite kind, winter-white calvilles.
The scales were broken and they didn't register.
The fluorescent vacuum showed a couple of grams
so the grocer smiled and frowned and said *Humph. A miracle.*
Sí, un milagro. A new start every year or so
because you and I keep on getting it wrong...
Oh happy error, I sing for the last few blocks,
the weightless apples floating in my hands.

THE SAME POEM, MOVING BACKWARDS
THROUGH TIME

We were talking about childhood punishment:
'I only remember once being spanked,'
I recalled. 'We were going to the Botanic Gardens;
I hid under the bed when we were about to leave.'
James Brydon interrupted: 'Who the fuck are you? Marcel Proust?'
Small coloured birds move active through the undergrowth.

Small coloured birds move active through the undergrowth.
We were discussing childhood punishments.
and James Brydon scoffed—'Who are you, Swinburne?'—
when I remembered only being birched once:
'I hid under the ottoman when we were about to leave;
I recall that we were going to the Vauxhall Gardens.'

I remember we were headed for the Marylebone Gardens—
Small coloured birds moved active through the undergrowth—
I had tried, unsuccessfully, to hide under the commode.
We were conversing upon the chastisements of youth:
I said: 'I was only ever horsewhipped once.'
James Brydon ridiculed me: 'D—n your eyes! Are you Dr Johnson?'

James Brydon laughed: 'God's teeth! Art thou Lord Bacon?'
We were footing slow towards Finsbury Field,
and I had said that my sire beat me but once.
Small coloured birds move active through the undergrowth.
We discussed childhood, its punishments:
ere we embarked on our journey I had hidden in the clothes-press.

It befell that I did try to hide me in the rafters.
Quod Isaac Brydon: 'Thou clod, art thou Boethius?'
We talked of youth and its villainous bane,
as we did wend in pilgrimage to Canterbury.
Small coloured birds moved active through the undergrowth.
I suffered but once at my father's hand.

Only once did he raise his hand against me in anger,
for that I hid myself away in the coffin.
Small coloured birds moved active through the undergrowth.
Jakob Brydon said: 'Fool! Are you the sagawriter?
We took our way towards the Hangman's Rock,
and talked of the cruelty of childhood.

Is this a punishment; am I being chastised?
I am going to the Lawstone; I will hide there.
'Am I the Elohist?' I ask the small, coloured birds.

My wife just broke her little toe
kicking me on the shins.

What you lose on the roundabouts
you make back on the swings.

FROM MAYHEW

Yes, I make the detonating crackers,
and am the only man in England skilful to make them.
It live in my breast alone—the full entire secret.
I will show you the pulling crackers.
They go at the parties of the rich.

A gentleman says to a lady, please to pull,
and so the pretty lady pull,
and the cracker goes bang—a sudden bang—
and the lady goes Ah-h-h! *sudden too,*
though she must have known the crack was to come.

Before I vanish for good, my aim
is to become a perfect sphere,
and only then to wither
(marble, petit pois, sandgrain, atom)
until I completely disappear.
I sit curved over in my chair.

I perceive around me the electromagnetic ocean.

The word *reality* only signifies *strong belief*:
I forced myself from bed
at what I believed was sunrise,
and came to the sea.

She was talking—*it's you, I've always wanted you.*

I told you, didn't I, that I've learned to ignore her?
Dark blue young mother. I try to ignore her.
But again, in some moods, the sea is an oyster
clamping tight on her pearl.

Looking, still looking, and the sea still sorting.

It's you, I never wanted you.
The tideline—sticking plasters, old rope,
sea thistles, a pair of sunglasses, a single cast-off shoe.
All these abandoned, drowned,
mass-produced manmade products...

You'll notice I never write about my parents.

Here you see is the pedestal of a statue;
there were many here once.
I think it is a sign of human weakness
to try to find the shape and form of God,
though at times I have thought
the word was breathing, just like that.

The sea again, in case you don't remember:
I am not judging, I never judge; we're family.

STORM

I don't know how to talk to you
today I don't know how to talk
to you today I don't know how
to talk to you I don't know how to talk

I leave our bed, the sky is heavy with night
and a storm approaching,
though still a while away yet.
The sky occasionally blanching.

I go to piss, and yawn. In the street
a cat investigates our doorway,
rubs her nose at the porter's feet
then mews and runs away.

The angel of rubbish spreads her
wings over the one a.m. city.
You see what I'm doing here?
Come back to bed, come back honey.

And just before the wild
hail makes us all inaudible,
the refrigerator cries and gurgles
like somebody else's child.

PROMETHEUS

This is what must happen
when you marry fire
who steals your melting skin
as you hold onto her.

AFTER RILKE

Dude, time is up. The summer was a blast.
Throw down some shadows on the picket fence
and loose the breezes in the heavy grass.

There's just two weekends left till fall semester,
maybe a kegger on for throwback Thursday:
make the most of it, get there early, drink
the last cold truth amid the backwash and the suds.

Ain't joined a frat, boy? Ain't going to join a frat.
Ain't tapped that ass yet? That ain't gonna happen.
All-nighters, book reports and midterm papers;
criss-crossing campus with your dorky rucksack
uncertain, while the leaves turn certain red.

CAUCASIAN MELODIES

for John Ash, with respect

Whoever could have imagined that music was
'about' anything? But the one tune
that everybody in our country knew had colours
and a protagonist, even

if it had no words. I am coming from there.
What could I do? That is
why there are traces of tears on my face.

FIREWORKS IN ZAKAMENSK

for Shoël Stadlen

Shoël and I, roving Siberia in search of shamans,
were misled south by a dead American
and ended up down in Zakamensk—
former Molybdenum Capital of the Buryat Republic!

On the way on the train a man with a beard
trapped us into conversation and gave us a firework.
He was writing a book and showed us the manuscript:
the Acknowledgements page said, 'No, *you* should thank *me*.'

Way down south in Zakamensk (FMCBR!)
we got a flat from the mayor, or a cousin of the mayor's,
eight dollars a night from a friend of a cousin—
fleeing water and enough furniture for one of us.

A day or so, a day or part of a day,
we drove the uncanny valley looking for shamans.
At night we invaded the pitch-black tiers—
concrete, abandoned—of the football pitch.

Back at the place we had taken for home
we decided to let off (pardon?) let off the firework.
A firework, firecracker, small bomb, bomblet,
the shape, more or less, of the Soyuz-U2 rocket.

We lit the little fuse and stood well back.
No illumination but a huge explosion.
We laughed and we laughed until the lights went on
in angry flats around the tussocky courtyard.

We only found one or two shamans,
and the next day thought it better to leave town.
But for a while back there we were history's actors
and you, all of you, will be left to study what we did.

BALANCE

It didn't want to let the morning
come, as if the globe were rocking back,
back and forwards, twisting gently like
a fair-day weathervane, and turning
towards the sun, turning us away.
Calm but firm, the world like a mother
did not allow it to be either
one thing or the other, night or day.
The sky was gritty with darkness, with
the light and the dark mixed, for the air
was full of masonry-dust, plaster,
powder, snowflakes, soot. I thought that if
I tore the page off the calendar
the next page would have the same number.
It didn't want to let morning come.
Fine by us. But the mechanism
slips suddenly out of gear – we are
jerked forward, lose balance once more.
This is the first station of autumn—
the sun is up, the scales have fallen.

BEHEADING VIDEOS

by now you have seen it all
no need to imagine it unimaginable kneeling
on a clay floor raised up   *sursum*
for the ease of the slaughterman
in falling them and for laying them
to bleed more freely   *meekly kneeling*
when they observe the sun rise and set
they utter terrible curses against it
the cause of disaster   *cometh as a whirlwind*
nor do they dream like the rest of mankind
for their calamity shall rise suddenly

when only touch remains do the fingers register and value every
        grain of sand

now you have all seen it
now you have seen it all   *click away click away*
find something else for your absent minutes
oh so the slo-mo video
a golf ball splatting into steel plate
golf ball golf pancake golf strawberry   *dimpled heart*

...à changer mon pot de chambre en un vase de parfum.

Marcel Proust, *Du côté de chez Swann*

Spargelpisse, which took me back to Germany,
white and green asparagus laid out in a Munich market,
extravagantly-priced bundles of sticks.
I turned them to watery risotto for our hosts:
we slept in their bed, they slept on a couch in the corridor,
when I did the washing-up I broke most of their possessions.
My dear, the *noise*, and the *people*! And the smell...
I stood by the sink, looking at the little fragments
which took me back to a month or so in St. Petersburg,
one of *those* months, totalled, dead in unlust,
an older German woman, with another life
manifest in her sudden absences, trips to the south.
She brought back tiny delicate vodka-cups from Elista,
and one morning we woke up to desolation.
Tja. Breaking these unnecessary fragile things.
Memory is a kind of heredity, which took me back to
a photo she described to me once, her and her cousins
in a cornfield, all of them tall with cornblond hair.
Na ja she said, thoughtfully. *Not good.*

Empirically-minded little bastard,
he's stamping on the cracks between the stones.
A stamp, a pause, he looks around. 'No bears.
No bears, papa!' Of course there are no bears.
It's quiet today, the police have shotguns
as Oliver and I walk slowly to the market.
He's laughing: I don't really want to laugh;
he glances slanting and hangs from my arm.
I caught on TV this morning half a sentence
of unwitting metre, a lop-eared alexandrine:
We may not know exactly who we need to kill...
Now I think about it, a complete sentence:
it doesn't matter who was speaking.
Oliver wants to watch a street magician
hide himself in a box and disappear.
A good trick if you can sell it: mirrors?
Mass hypnosis? I'd like to know, today of all days.
'Come on now, Ol, there's no time, we're busy.'
There is time, but crowds make me uneasy.
A police car driven through the crowd,
clicking like a gunmetal dolphin.
Everything uncomfortable, the world
slightly at a slant to itself, balancing
on its own edge. You feel you need to be ready.
Oliver impatient now, pulls at my sleeve,
a pivot against the news dragging me outwards.
The necessary anchor. 'Papa, papa!'
He's pleased with himself; he's worked it all out.
'Papa, papa!' The self-belief of childhood,
unaware of the joy it inflicts on others.
'Papa, papa!' 'What is it?' 'Papa, no bears!'
I lie and say: 'You're right. No bears. No bears.'

November 2015. Europe

EUROPE

When at the turn of the year over the beaten down continent,
the homeland of turmoil, of brotherly hatred, of insurgency, of sin,
the homeland of bold thoughts, of burning words, of beauty,
when at the turn of the year the bells ring out, bells that have come
    home,
have been heaved to the top of failing towers
the great bells—
when the high foehn-driven water roars to fill the space under
    bridges,
when the trains pipe up and the ships sound their bustling sirens,
when the unknown voice calls *Happy New Year* up to the silent
    window,

then a heart will bow to its beloved, will whisper almost silently
Love me for ever, for all the days to come,
and will be snatched away by the bell-wind, storm-wind,
over the boundaries of itself, high over the city,
over the silent countries,

and will hear prayers and many prophecies, which arise
and call out the day when peace will be plenty,
when the righteous man will flourish,
when the outlaw will be gone, his lair impossible to find.
And they speak, of a seed that will grow up golden from the bodies
    of the dead,
of gardens which flourish without walls and which will bear fruit,
of a single world where no one knows fear,
of eternal peace.

But there is another prediction, taken ancient from Nostradamus,
of horses from Asia going down to drink from the Rhine,
of a bloody river that must flow before the kingdom does come,
of cities that must crumble and fields that must be made desert
      before
the kingdom comes,
of armies that will burst from the east and from the west in fury
and clash like the waves of the spring tide, in violence,
and pull back away from each other like waves of the spring tide.
But where they have been, is dead.
It is steppe, where they have been, bee-buzzing,
no-man's-land, primeval—

and this is where he aims, the dream wanderer, with the bell-wind,
      storm-wind,
over the shuddering continent,
the homeland of turmoil, of brotherly hatred, of insurgency, of sin,
the homeland of bold thoughts, of burning words, of beauty.
He tastes again the coasts at Brittany's margin,
where laurel and rose bend in the Atlantic gales,
down to the waters of the Golden Horn, from Midgard
to the Pillars of Hercules.

And a shape out of time hurtles towards him, nightmare ghosts
      from the Elbe,
girls with wings like swans, Poseidon's black steed,
and he sees castles, sees temples and cloisters, vaulted roofs, palaces,
and always the ploughman in the fields at autumn and always
armies on the march, bearing weapons.

And voices rise up to him, fervent choruses,
demanding joy and demanding love and always
and always the same sullen terribly abandoned voice,
the voice of Prometheus.

But then it calms down.
Calm in the moonlight, under broken clouds
there flourish for him once more the sweet things, the saved
        things—
the marble joys of Vicenza, Roman fountains,
the lovely foolish virgins on Freiburg cathedral,
the Chartres rose and Goethe's garden by the river Stern.

And he thinks he has never seen it so beautiful, so full of promises.
And he thinks his eyes are brighter than a mourner's eyes,
and his hands are stronger than a mourner's hands,
and he thinks his own heart is full of life.

And he wants to cry out, shout into the world, looking for
        something solid,
so that not for the sake of peace,
not for the sake of one who will come
not for this will they strangle, put out
the happiness of the eyes,
the freedom of the spirit,
the upheaval of the heart,
the same old lonely voice
of the watcher in his tower.

He cries out, he cries out into the world, the dream wanderer,
but no answer sounds back to him. Only the bells,
that sing storm and sing peace,
sing death and sing Noël,
the mysterious inexplicable bells
still call
midnight—

and yet, when he goes home sad and bows once again
and whispers again his *Love me for all the days to come*,
the heart of his heart has long since stepped over the edge of the
      year,
eternally consoled
with its small perpetual beating.

after the German of Marie Luise Kaschnitz

ON TRUST

I ask you
to take all this

Notes

The Colonel's statement about his stories is something my father told me once.

An *aisling* is originally an Irish poetic genre: it is a form of dream vision, in which the poet sees a woman who represents Ireland, and who informs him of the future of his country. As is clear, I have adapted it for my own selfish ends.

'256 Poems of Love and Regret' is a set of four sonnets designed to be able to be divided up and read in any order, the first quatrain of one, the closing couplet of another &c. &c. Provoking the same emotions by the use of different combinations of words, perhaps.

'error' is a translation of the short prose text 'error' by the contemporary Russian poet Marianna Geide. It comes from her prose collection *Мертвецкий фонарь* (2007).

'From Mayhew' is an adaptation of a report I found in *The Unknown Mayhew: Selections from the* Morning Chronicle *1849–50*.

'From Rilke' is an extremely free translation of Rilke's 'Herbsttag', first collected in *Das Buch der Bilder* (1902).

'Europe' is a translation of Marie Luise Kaschnitz's poem 'Europa' which I found in Patrick Bridgwater, ed., *Twentieth-Century German Verse*.

This is a book of lies; these notes are true.